Jacques Cousteau

Free Flight
Undersea

by Paul Westman
Illustrated by Reg Sandland

DILLON PRESS, INC. MINNEAPOLIS, MINNESOTA

Library of Congress Cataloging in Publication Data

Westman, Paul.
    Jacques Cousteau, free flight undersea.

    (Taking Part; 8)
    SUMMARY: A biography of the French oceanographer
whose underwater explorations have focused the
world's attention on the beauty of ocean life and the
need to conserve that life.
    1. Cousteau, Jacques Yves—Juvenile literature.
    2. Oceanographers—France—Biography—Juvenile
literature.
    [1. Cousteau, Jacques Yves. 2. Oceanographers] I.
Sandland, Reg. II. Title.
    GC30.C68W47   551.4'6'00924 [B] [92]   79-22232

    ISBN 0-87518-188-0

Dillon Press, Inc., 500 South Third Street
Minneapolis, Minnesota 55415

Printed in the United States of America
4 5 6 7 8 9 10 11 12 92 91 90 89 88 87 86 85 84

JACQUES COUSTEAU

Born in France, Jacques Cousteau revolutionized undersea exploration by inventing and perfecting the Aqua-lung and the diving saucer. He served in the French navy and won the Legion of Honor for his daring missions in the French Underground during World War II. Later he explored the oceans of the world on his famous ship, the *Calypso*. Cousteau has won three Academy Awards for his undersea films and has written several books about sea life. His story reveals not only the beauty of ocean life, but also the need to conserve the ocean's resources.

Jacques-Yves Cousteau was born on June 11, 1910, in a country town in France. The town, Saint-André-de-Cubzac, is near the port of Bordeaux.

Jacques's father, Daniel Cousteau, was a lawyer. He worked for an American millionaire. The millionaire traveled a great deal. The Cousteaus traveled with him. They rarely stayed in any one place long. In fact, the first thing Jacques can remember was being rocked to sleep on a train.

The only time the Cousteaus were not on the move was in the summer. Summers they spent at a seaside home in Royan, France.

Although he was a thin, frail lad, Jacques refused to behave like one. He stayed active and busy. At Royan he played and swam in the Atlantic Ocean. Here he developed his lifelong love for the sea.

When Jacques was ten, the Cousteaus moved to
New York City for a year. Jacques's new friends
quickly gave him the nickname "Jack." Together
Jacques and his friends played baseball, built snow
forts, and went to school. Soon Jacques's English
was almost perfect. Still, he never lost his heavy
French accent.

Jacques spent part of that year at a summer camp in Vermont. By this time he was a very good swimmer. One of the counselors noticed this. He asked Jacques if he would clear out some branches beneath the diving board by the lake. The branches were 12 feet underwater.

Jacques agreed. He dove into the water. Soon all of the branches had been cleared away.

That year the Cousteaus returned to France. Jacques kept on moving from school to school. Perhaps the constant changes were one of the reasons Jacques was such a poor student. Schoolwork bored him. Often he would get into mischief. He was expelled from one French school after breaking seventeen windows.

But Jacques was far from stupid. He just had to learn to apply himself. Later he became a top student.

Besides swimming, one of Jacques's favorite things to do was inventing. When he was 11, he built a 4-foot high model of an ocean crane. Mr. Cousteau showed the model to an engineer he knew.

"Your son has built a perfect scale model of the crane," the engineer said. "But he has also added a new part which makes the crane work better. He could even patent it."

Another of Jacques's inventions was an electric car. He built the car when he was 13.

Jacques also enjoyed making motion pictures. He saved long and hard to buy his own movie

camera. As soon as he got it, he took it apart to see what made it run.

Soon Jacques's parents allowed him to go on vacations alone. He visited England, Spain, and Germany. On these trips he learned a great deal about foreign languages and customs.

After high school Jacques decided to become a sailor. He enrolled at Stanislas College in Paris. Stanislas prepared students for the French Naval Academy. The academy, in turn, trained young men to become officers in the French navy.

Jacques was one of the best students at Stanislas. No longer did he neglect his schoolwork. But he found some time to have fun, too. For one thing, he played rugby on the school team. Rugby is a European sport much like football.

Jacques had no trouble getting into the naval academy. His grades at Stanislas were very good.

Academy training took place both in the class-room and on board ship. Part of the training in-cluded a year-long cruise around the world. Jacques's ship visited Arabia, Borneo, and San Francisco.

Cousteau graduated from the naval academy in 1933. He ranked second in a class of 1000. First the navy sent him to command its base in Shanghai, China. Then it sent him on a map-making survey along the Indochina coast. After the survey Cousteau returned to France.

One night he was driving his sports car along a foggy mountain road. Suddenly he lost control of the car. It plunged off the road and tumbled down a steep hill.

Minutes later Jacques opened his eyes. He was in terrible pain. Both his arms were broken. If he did not get help soon, he would die. He dragged himself to a darkened cottage. Luckily, someone there sent for help.

One of Jacques's arms was infected. "We are sorry," Cousteau's doctors told him, "but the arm must be removed."

Jacques refused to hear of such a thing. "No," he replied firmly.

He could not move his arm even one inch. Day after day he worked at making his arm well again. After eight months he managed to wiggle one finger. It seemed like a miracle, but soon his whole arm was moving again.

When at last he was fit for duty, Jacques was stationed at Toulon on the Mediterranean Sea in southern France. He spent part of each day in the water. Swimming helped strengthen his weakened arms.

One day a friend showed him a pair of goggles. The goggles allowed divers to see clearly under-water. Pearl divers in the South Seas had used such

goggles for many years. In Europe and America though, they were almost unknown.

On a warm day in 1936, Cousteau tried the goggles for the first time. He went to a beach on the edge of town and waded into the water. Pulling the goggles over his eyes, he ducked his head into the sea.

The water was crystal clear and filled with sea life. There were fish of every shape and size. Brown,

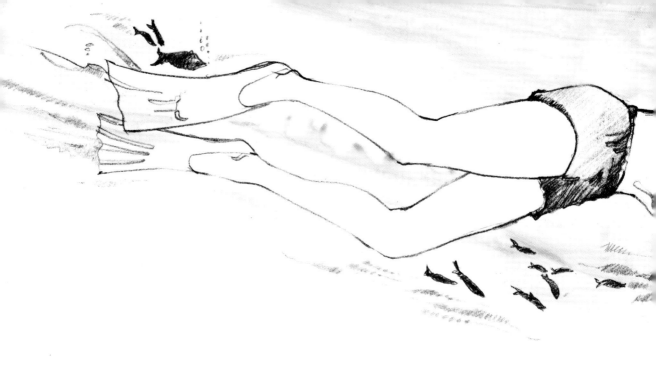

green, and silver rocks stretched out along the sea bottom.

Cousteau raised his head out of the water. He was in the everyday world again. The sun shone brightly. People played on the crowded beach. A streetcar clanged. Amazed, he plunged his head into the water once more. He had discovered a whole new world.

From that moment on, Cousteau knew exactly what he wanted to do. He wanted to explore the sea.

At that time deep sea diving was almost unheard of. Diving suits were bulky and dangerous. The

diver's head was encased in a heavy steel helmet. Air
flowed to the helmet through a hose attached to the
deck of a ship. The hose did not allow much freedom
of movement. If the hose got tangled or cut, the diver
could drown.

Cousteau wanted to find a way to make diving
easier and safer. The goggles helped. Soon he added
rubber fins as well. With the fins on his feet, he could
move through the water at far greater speed. A small
piece of hose to breathe through helped, too. In this

way Cousteau found that he could swim on the surface with his head underwater. Soon he learned to dive to great depths without any breathing equipment at all.

But even this did not satisfy him. He built a device made of tanks of pure oxygen to breathe underwater. He did not know that breathing oxygen underwater was dangerous. Twice he was almost killed when his body began to shake violently.

These underwater tests were stopped by World War II. In the early part of the war, Cousteau served as an officer aboard the warship *Dupleix.* Then the Germans attacked France. Before long they took over the whole country. The French navy was sunk to keep it from falling into German hands.

Cousteau was transferred to a fort along the French coast. Without ships naval officers had little to do. Once more Jacques explored the ocean depths. At this time there was a food shortage. The Germans thought Cousteau was spearfishing to help make up for it. And he was. But he also watched the comings and goings of the German fleet.

Cousteau was a member of the French underground. The underground was a secret network of French patriots who fought and spied on the Germans. Many members of the underground lost their lives.

Cousteau took part in many secret missions. On one, dressed as an Italian officer, he slipped into enemy headquarters. With a tiny camera he photographed the Italian codebook and other top secret papers. After the war the French government

awarded Cousteau the Legion of Honor and the War Cross, two of its highest medals.

Still, he was drawn to the sea. Even during the war he spent every spare moment in the water. The Germans knew he was fooling around with tanks and other gadgets. But they just thought he was strange.

By now his dream of a lightweight breathing device was close to coming true.

This is how it would work. Two tanks filled with compressed air would be strapped to a diver's back. A hose would carry the air from the tanks to the diver's mouth. A valve would control the flow of air.

Cousteau did not have the know-how to build such a valve. He asked a Paris engineer, Emile Gagnan, to help him. Gagnan was able to produce just what Cousteau needed. The breathing device was complete!

Cousteau called his invention the Aqua-lung. The Aqua-lung is the breathing equipment used by all scuba divers today. Before Cousteau's invention scuba diving did not exist.

In June 1943, Cousteau tested the Aqua-lung. His wife Simone floated on the surface above him. If

something went wrong, she would signal to a man onshore. The man would dive down and rescue Cousteau before he drowned.

But nothing went wrong. Cousteau waded out to sea. He ducked beneath the surface. The white sand floor slanted into the clear blue distance. Rays of sunlight shone through the water. The undersea world was silent and peaceful.

To test his new underwater freedom, Cousteau sped through the water like a fish. He glided like a bird in free flight. He did somersaults. He stood upside down on one finger. And he wanted to shout for joy.

After the war Cousteau set up the Undersea Research Group. This was a new part of the French navy. Its members explored shipwrecks, took pictures, and carried out experiments.

The Undersea Research Group cleared away German mines in French waters. The mines were still active. If jarred, they would explode. Group divers also brought up bombs and torpedoes from the ocean floor.

One of their finds was a very old Roman ship. The ship had sunk in the Mediterranean around two

thousand years ago. The warlike Romans had used the ship to loot the art treasures of the Greeks.

Cousteau and his men spent six days exploring the wreck. The divers found iron and bronze nails and parts of an anchor. They even found a stone used by the ship's cook to grind grain for food. The wood from the ship was covered with yellow varnish. The purpose of the varnish was to protect the wood from the harsh salt water. And it had done just that—for two thousand years!

By this time Jacques and Simone had two sons.

Jean-Michel was seven. Philippe was five. Cousteau wanted his sons to learn how to dive. You do not have to know how to swim in order to scuba dive. You just have to be able to kick your feet and breathe air through a hose.

Jacques and his sons waded into the sea near their home. Jean-Michel and Philippe were excited. They opened their mouths to speak. They wanted to tell their father about all the wonderful things they saw underwater. Jacques had to swim from one to the other, putting the air hoses back in their mouths.

Even so, both Jean-Michel and Philippe became expert divers in just a short time.

Near the shore diving was safe. But deep sea diving could be dangerous.

One danger was rapture of the deep. Rapture overcame divers that swam too deep in the water. It made them do strange things.

Rapture caused some divers to think they were gods. Others ripped the air hoses from their mouths, thinking they could breathe water. Still others wanted to stay underwater forever.

Cousteau and his men feared rapture. They knew it could destroy their will to live.

Another danger was the high pressure at deep depths. The twin threats of rapture and high pressure made deep diving very risky.

Because of these dangers, no one knew just how far down divers could go. Cousteau decided there was only one way to find out. He would go down himself.

A long rope, marked at different depths, was lowered into the water. Boards were attached. Cousteau would mark the boards with a pencil to show how deep he had gone.

The deepest level any scuba diver had yet reached was 210 feet. This mark had been set by Cousteau's friend Frederic Dumas. At that depth Dumas had suffered rapture of the deep. Cousteau knew that a deeper dive would be dangerous.

On a bright, hot day in 1947, Cousteau leaped into the sea. Iron weights helped pull him under. Soon the sunlight vanished, and he was dropping through darkness.

At 200 feet down he was struck by rapture. He paused. Suddenly he was a child again, sick in bed. His head throbbed. His fingers seemed as thick as wooden pegs. At last he gained control of himself. He pushed on into deeper water.

Farther and farther he dropped. Visions danced before his eyes. An eerie glow surrounded him. The glow came from light shining on the ocean floor. Cousteau dropped to the very end of the rope, just above the sea floor. He wrote his name on the board.

Then he dropped the weights and soared upward. As he rose at high speed, he saw the surface "in a

blaze of bubbles and dancing prisms." Cousteau had reached a depth of 300 feet. This was deeper than humans had ever gone before during a free dive.

One of the toughest divers in Cousteau's crew was a Frenchman named Maurice Fargues. A short time after Cousteau's feat, Fargues made a dive of his own.

During the dive the rope went slack. Quickly the men on board ship hauled the Frenchman to the surface. But it was too late. He was already dead. Rapture had pulled the air hose from his mouth. Later the men found his name marked on a board 400 feet down.

Sharks were another danger of the sea. In the 1940s not much was known about them. Cousteau and his men believed sharks would only attack divers floating on the surface. But one close call led them to be more careful.

Cousteau and Frederic Dumas were taking under-water pictures with a movie camera. When a shark appeared, they were not frightened. They had met other sharks in the water.

Cousteau and Dumas swam toward the shark. When it did not swim away, they were surprised. Dumas played with the shark while Cousteau took pictures. Dumas swam in front of the shark and behind it. He even grabbed the shark's tail. Suddenly two more sharks appeared. Each one was 15 feet long.

Now Cousteau and Dumas were worried. If they swam to the surface, the sharks might attack them. If they stayed below, they would run out of air.

The men tried every trick they knew to scare the sharks away. They hooted through their masks. They waved their arms. They blew bubbles. Nothing worked.

The first shark turned and glided straight at them. It came so close that Cousteau had to bang it on the snout with his camera. After pausing, it backed away.

The two men had to risk going up for help. When they reached the surface, they waved their arms. Since the ship was far away, no one saw them. The sharks prepared to attack. Quickly the men dove back down. Time after time, they rose up and then dove down again. Cousteau and Dumas were growing dizzy. They were cold and tired and their air was running out. Soon they would be eaten alive.

Suddenly a shadow fell across them. The sharks vanished. The shadow belonged to a small boat. Someone on the ship had finally seen them. From that day on, Dumas and Cousteau were more careful of sharks.

Cousteau had long dreamed of owning a ship of his own. In 1950 he found such a ship, The *Calypso*. A wealthy friend of Cousteau's helped pay for it. Cousteau made the *Calypso* into the most up-to-date research ship afloat.

The *Calypso's* sailors searched shipwrecks, made underwater movies, and looked for oil. They studied every type of marine life they could find. No adventure was too big for them to tackle.

By the 1950s scuba diving had become a popular sport. Cousteau had opened a new frontier for humankind. But now many people had explored the coastal waters. It was time for pioneers such as Cousteau to move on. The new frontier was the ocean floor, where scuba divers could not go.

In the 1940s Cousteau had helped Professor Auguste Piccard test the first bathyscaphe. The bathyscaphe was a round, undersea vessel large enough for two people. This vessel could withstand great pressure. It could be lowered deeper than any human could swim.

A second bathyscaphe, called *FNRS 3*, dropped a mile below the surface. As it went down, the water changed from green, to blue, to black. Cousteau switched on the outside lights. The dark waters lit up with a dazzling brilliance.

At first it seemed to be snowing. Thousands of white "flakes" floated past the window. The oddest thing of all was that the flakes were falling up!

Of course, it was not really snowing. The flakes were really tiny forms of sea life. Nor were they

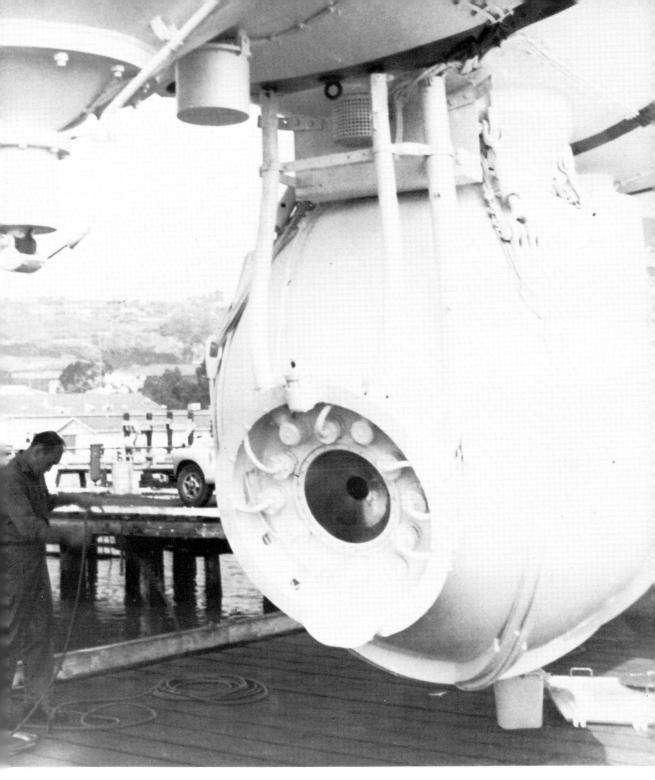

Bathyscaphes like the one shown here make it possible to explore the ocean floor.

falling upward. It only seemed as if they were because the bathyscaphe was dropping down.

Large squid with their long tentacles hung in the green silence. There were other fish, too. Many of them were unknown to humans. They had never been seen before.

The lights were turned off. The bathyscaphe, far beneath the surface, was plunged into darkness. But all around it tiny animals glowed. Some flashed through the sea like comets across the night sky.

Bathyscaphe dives such as this convinced Cousteau that deep diving was important. One day, he believed, deep dives would gather food, metal, and other resources from the ocean depths. As the world's population grew, land resources would be used up. Humans would have no choice but to go beneath the sea.

But Cousteau knew these were only dreams. Much work was needed to make the dreams come true. Many things had to be learned. Could a person live for a long time underwater? Could the human body put up with the hardships of the deep sea?

To find the answers, Cousteau launched a series of bold experiments. The experiments were called Conshelf I, Conshelf II, and Conshelf III. They took place in 1961, 1963, and 1965.

During the Conshelf tests, men lived in underwater houses for days or weeks at a time. The Conshelf tests were the first attempts by humans to live underwater. Captain Cousteau directed the tests. Often he visited his men underwater. But he did not take part himself.

Conshelf I was an underwater house shaped like a big barrel. It was anchored to the sea floor by heavy

weights. For seven days two divers lived in Conshelf
I. All this time they stayed at the bottom of the sea.

*The Cousteau diving saucer (center) was used by the divers
in Conshelf II.*

Conshelf II was an underwater village. It was made up of four houses instead of just one. Seven men lived in Conshelf II for an entire month. It was lowered to the bottom of the Red Sea near the coast of Africa. Many sharks lived in these waters.

Conshelf II had a large house for divers to live in, a garage for a diving saucer, a tool shed, and a "deep station." The deep station was deeper in the water than the other buildings. Two men could swim down to it and live apart from the others for days at a time.

The men made a film of their stay at Conshelf II. The film was *World Without Sun*. It won an Academy Award.

The last experiment was Conshelf III. Conshelf III was the boldest test of all. In it six men spent three weeks beneath the sea. More important, they lived at a depth far deeper than anyone had lived before.

Captain Cousteau was pleased by the results of the three Conshelf experiments. They brought human-kind one step closer to being able to live and work in the sea.

In 1956 Cousteau had resigned from the French navy to become a full-time explorer. Over the years many groups helped pay for his voyages. Cousteau's own books and films helped pay for the voyages, too. These books and films made him famous the world over.

Cousteau wrote many books describing his adventures. All of them have beautiful color pictures. These pictures give readers a glimpse of life beneath the sea. Two of his most popular books are *The Silent World* and *The Living Sea.* Thousands of copies have been sold.

Millions more have seen Cousteau's underwater films. Many of these films were shown on TV as specials. Others were used on his two TV series, "The Undersea World of Jacques Cousteau" and "The Cousteau Odyssey."

In 1972 Captain Cousteau and the *Calypso* explored the Antarctic Ocean. Here the *Calypso* performed many tests. The data it gathered was sent to the United States by satellite. The men were surprised to find lots of sea life in the cold Antarctic waters.

Crew members made many dives. Wetsuits protected them from the icy water. The men swam like fish in and around huge icebergs. Eerie caverns gleamed beneath the waters. Cracks like rifle shots echoed through the sea. At any moment the ice could break, trapping the divers below. In spite of the danger, the men carried out their mission.

On another trip Cousteau and his crew searched for a famous shipwreck.

Most people have heard of the *Titanic*. The *Titanic* was the largest and finest ocean liner of its day. It was thought to be unsinkable. Then, on its first voyage in 1912, it struck an iceberg and sank. This was one of the greatest shipwrecks in history.

The story of the *Britannic* is not so well known. The *Britannic* was built at the same time as the

Titanic. In fact, the *Britannic* was the *Titanic's* sister ship. It, too, was thought to be unsinkable. Then, in 1916, it exploded and sank. No one knew what caused the explosion.

In 1977 the *Calypso's* crew found the lost wreck of the *Britannic.* Cousteau and his men made many dives to try to find out why it sank. They did find some clues. Still, they weren't able to tell for sure what caused the ship to go down.

Next the crew searched for the lost island of Atlantis. Atlantis is famous in myth and legend. Old records state that it sank into the sea thousands of years ago. Many people have tried to find traces of the fabled island. Cousteau's crew tried, too, but they didn't find anything. The undersea city is still a mystery.

On most of his trips, Cousteau was aided by his son Philippe. Philippe was a grown man now. Like his father, he was a full-time explorer aboard the *Calypso.* He helped photograph and produce many of his father's TV shows.

Then, in the summer of 1979, Philippe was

Philippe Cousteau joined his father as a full-time explorer aboard the Calypso.

killed. A plane he was flying crashed in a river in Portugal. A few days later he was buried at sea. Philippe's death was a great loss for Jacques and Simone.

In recent years Cousteau has turned his attention to the problem of pollution. He believes that this problem is a threat to all people on earth. Pollution is killing the oceans.

Cousteau has been diving for 40 years. He, more than anyone, knows how badly polluted the oceans have become. Sometimes he returned to places where he had dived years before. Water that had once been crystal clear and full of life was now foul and dead.

"All pollution ends up in the sea," he says. "The earth is less polluted. It is washed by the rain which carries everything into the oceans."

Nearly half the life in the sea has been killed by pollution during Cousteau's lifetime alone. Most countries have done little to try to stop pollution. In fact, each year they make it worse. They do not seem to worry about the future of the oceans.

Oil spills from ships such as the Argo Merchant *threaten sea life in the oceans of the world.*

Jacques Cousteau is convinced that people must take the first step themselves. He believes that working together, people can show governments that pollution must be stopped.

To help, he formed the Cousteau Society. The Cousteau Society works through the United Nations and world governments for strict antipollution laws.

Although he's 70 years old now, Jacques Cousteau has no thoughts of slowing down. He is as active as ever, diving, speaking, and traveling. Often he travels 100,000 miles in a year. He owns two houses but rarely lives in them. Most of the time he is aboard the *Calypso*. And the *Calypso*, like its captain, is always on the move.

"I think life is terribly short," Cousteau once told a reporter. "I would like to do more with these few years I have on earth. So I have to hurry up."

The Author

Paul Westman is a regular contributor to *Current Biography* and has written many books for young people, including several for the Taking Part series. Of the series, Westman says, "Young readers will learn something about well-known contemporary men and women in many challenging fields and at the same time begin to discover some of the joys of reading."

A recent graduate of the University of Minnesota, Westman lives in Minneapolis.

The Illustrator

Reg Sandland is a freelance illustrator and graphic designer whose work has appeared in numerous newspapers and magazines, as well as one previous book. He is a graduate of Bemidji State University and has attended the University of Minnesota and the Minneapolis College of Art and Design.

Photographs reproduced through the courtesy of KTCA-TV, St. Paul, Minnesota, the Minneapolis Public Library, and the United States Navy.